A TASTE OF CHICKEN SOUP TO INSPIRE A WOMAN'S SOUL

Stories Celebrating the Wisdom, Fun and Freedom of Midlife

Jack Canfield
Mark Victor Hansen
Stephanie Marston

Health Communications, Inc.
Deerfield Beach, Florida

www.bcibooks.com
www.chickensoup.com

Library of Congress Cataloging-in-Publication Data is available from the Library of Congress

©2005 Jack Canfield and Mark Victor Hansen
ISBN 0-7573-0502-4

Publisher: Health Communications Inc.,
3201 SW 15th Street, Deerfield Beach, FL 33442

This book is dedicated to the millions of midlife women who dare to take time to nurture their souls and open their hearts fully to life.

Contents

Introduction

This book is a gift to you, the midlife women of the world. Women in our culture often struggle to focus on themselves, their needs and their dreams. Let's face it, much of women's value comes from the ability to know what other people's needs are and to fulfill them. Yet, deep within, each woman longs to reinstate herself at the center of her own life.

Don't panic: We're not suggesting that you abandon your family, career or loved ones. We're simply suggesting that you bring yourself back into the equation, that you make your needs part of the overall picture.

Let us let you in on a little secret: If you use this time to reevaluate your life—to question anything you've been doing on autopilot for a long time, be it in your career, family or relationships—then you can begin to unearth the secret wishes that will take you back to a more authentic sense of yourself.

Now's the time to take your neglected dreams off of the back burner. Whatever you've been longing to do, whatever you've been yearning to reclaim, now's the time.

The stories you are about to enjoy were originally published in *Chicken Soup to Inspire a Woman's Soul*. As you immerse yourself in these stories, we hope that you will explore your own quest for greater satisfaction and fulfillment.

The question remains: How can you make this time of your life rich in self-discovery, growth and transformation? To start, you can honor where you have been and what you've done; you can acknowledge the challenges you have endured, the strengths you have accumulated, and the knowledge you have extracted from your experiences. In other words, you can celebrate all that you are and all that you are becoming.

May you experience the inspiration, support and encouragement you need to discover greater passion, joy and fulfillment, and to make this time one of the best times of your life.

Dare To . . .

Ask for what you want.
Believe in yourself.
Change your mind.
Do what you love.
Enjoy each and every day.
Follow your heart's desire.
Give more than you receive.
Have a sense of humor.
Insist on being yourself.
Join in more.
Kiss and make up.
Love and be loved.
Make new friends.
Nurture your spirit.
Overcome adversity.
Play more.

Question conformity.
Reach for the stars.
Speak your truth.
Take personal responsibility.
Understand more, judge less.
Volunteer your time.
Walk through fear.
Xperience the moment.
Yearn for grace.
be Zany.

Meiji Stewart

Paper Suits Me

The big question is whether you are going to be able to say a hearty yes to your adventure.

Joseph Campbell

During the sweltering summer of 1990, my husband, Paul, booked a hotel in Thunder Bay, Canada, that had a giant waterslide in the pool area.

Our four children screamed when they saw it. They got on their swimming suits, walked around the waterslide, and counted the ten twists and turns. I sat happily at a table with four-year-old Colleen on my lap.

"Can Colleen go down the slide with me?" Anne, our oldest at twelve, asked me.

"How can she?"

"On my lap. I'll hang on to her."

Anne took her hand as they headed for the stairs. Clare and Erin, our middle two, followed right behind.

"Be careful," I yelled.

Anne and Colleen had just finished the slide. Anne landed standing up as she lifted her sister into the air. Since there was no splash, not even a drop of water fell onto our youngest daughter's hair.

I was beginning to wish I hadn't forgotten my swimming suit. It just looked like so much fun. Like Colleen, I had never gone down a waterslide. But unlike the rest of my family, I was afraid of the water.

"Why didn't I bring my swimming suit?" I asked my husband.

"Are you thinking about going down the slide?"

"Maybe."

"Go to the front desk and see if they sell any," Paul said.

I couldn't wonder any longer. I went to the front desk.

"Ma'am, um, this might sound like a weird question, but do you sell any swimming suits?"

"Sure do. They're ten dollars," the woman behind the desk said.

"Great." I couldn't believe my luck.

"One piece or two, Hon?"

"One is fine." My bikini days had gone by the wayside after four pregnancies, stretch marks, and permanent weight gain. "What material are they made of?"

"Paper," the woman said.

Paper? The image I had of myself catapulting down the slide as my suit disintegrated was frightening to say the least. "That's okay," I said as I started walking away from the desk.

"They're very strong, Ma'am."

"Strong enough for a waterslide?"

"Yes. Look." She took the suit and pulled at the seams. The stitches didn't budge.

"Okay, I guess I'll try it," I said, as I handed over a ten-dollar bill.

I went back to the room and changed into my paper suit. I inspected the texture again. It seemed strong, more like a heavy linen than paper. Just in case of any rupture, though, I wore a T-shirt over it.

"I'm ready," I said when I arrived at the pool.

My family was waiting to escort me to the

steps going up to the waterslide. There were two girls in front of me and two others bringing up the rear. Paul was in the pool, anticipating my landing.

"How do you slow down?" I kept asking.

No one answered. My children glanced at each other. The eye contact with me was non-existent.

We made it up the probably fifty steps without mishap. I didn't realize it was so high until I got to the top.

The line moved rapidly.

Anne and Colleen departed.

It was my turn now. No one was in front of me. The pounding in my chest let me know my heart was still beating.

"Do I sit?"

The attendant nodded his head.

I sat waiting for my signal to go. I swallowed the modest amount of saliva left in my mouth.

"How do you slow down?" I asked.

He looked at me strangely and said, "Just sit up straight."

"Okay," I said. I was sitting up straighter already.

"Go." The man motioned to me.

"ME? Right now?"

I was starting to sweat, but it wasn't from the heat. I looked at the long line behind me and decided it would be more embarrassing crawling over strangers and family than drowning in the three feet of water at the end.

"Lady, you can go."

I heard the words as I gingerly pushed myself down the slide.

I approached the first curve. I realized quickly and astutely that I had no control in the curves at all. I thought about swearing and then, luckily, thought again. I knew the words would echo and reverberate throughout the slide. My children would probably be traumatized for life.

I was going too fast.

Maybe if I put my legs up along the sides more, I'll slow down, I thought.

I did seem to slow down a fraction of a second. I knew I had to concentrate the entire length of the slide. The man had told me not to put my hands on the sides; I tried to keep them on my thighs, although I needed them for balance.

The bottom of my paper suit seemed to be filling with water but I didn't dare try to get it out. I pictured myself careening to the top of a curve, hanging suspended for a split second, and plopping down on my side. Or worse, I could flip over and land on my face with the water rushing up my nose.

Don't worry about the water, I told myself, as my buttocks swung from side to side.

I was weighing more with each passing second.

Paul said he would be waiting at the end for me. I hoped he planned to catch me and keep me from going under water. I went around the S-shaped curve and saw the opening that signaled the end of the slide. I wanted to land without so much as a ripple, as Anne and Colleen had. I saw my husband standing in the water. That was my last conscious sight before feeling my body fly through the air. I hit the surface, water-filled buttocks first, with a large splash as my face and every other part of me went completely under. I was still trying to stand when my husband grabbed my arm and pulled me up.

"Are you okay?" he said.

There was a mixture of laughter and clapping around the pool.

"I'm okay," I said. "I can't believe how fast it

is." I stated this fact loudly, so everyone could hear. "I felt like a rocket on that last curve."

"Mom, are you going again?" little Colleen asked.

There are some experiences in life that truly are "once is not enough." How could I say no to a four-year-old when she was almost jumping up and down?

"I think I'll go again," I said. I went back to the steps, and one of my daughters shielded me while I let out the ten pounds of water collected at the bottom of my suit. First the one side, then the other. I felt lighter already.

When the poor man saw me, he was too polite to let out a groan. And when he said go, I went. The third time I actually landed feet first, toes touching the bottom of the pool.

There was more applause from the bystanders.

After my tenth slide down, I decided to quit. The paper suit was miraculously still intact.

Paul told me later that all the people around the pool agreed that they had never seen a person go down a waterslide so slowly.

Mary Clare Lockman

The Piranha

You will do foolish things, but do them with enthusiasm.

Colette

My mother told me never to rock the boat or challenge a male authority figure.

"Men need to save face," she explained. "Conflict isn't worth it."

I took after my father. Opinionated, fearless, ready to crusade for justice.

I struggled with my natural gift of courage versus my desire to please Mom and never be pushy. As a result, I was always conflicted and guilt-ridden if I spoke up.

When my husband and I packed our few possessions and headed west to pursue our dreams of music, I would receive a lesson in assertiveness that would change me forever. Back in the Midwest, I sang local TV commercials. The prospect of finding work in Hollywood was frightening to say the least. For eight months, I mailed out demo tapes, called producers, dropped by studios and basically struck out. One day, I mailed my demo to a new production company.

They called me the very next day.

"We loved your tape!" the producer gushed. "Come to the studio Friday. There's a national TV commercial I want you to sing."

"Wow, that's great," I said.

"We can't pay you regular union rates, and you won't get future royalties, but I can guarantee one day of work a week at one hundred dollars an hour."

So that Friday, I sang the commercial, met the studio musicians and became a national "jingle singer."

Within weeks, I was their regular soloist and even sang backup with the other singers. The fact that we were grossly underpaid and signed agreements to waive all our royalties was okay with me. The hourly rate was more than I had ever earned in my life, and I was doing what I loved, so what did it matter?

Then reality hit.

My paycheck came in the mail every two weeks, and I kept perfect records about every recording session, but somehow the paychecks and my records would never coincide. The checks were always smaller than the amounts I showed being due. I kept "fluffing" it off thinking maybe I hadn't worked as many hours as I thought, figuring it must be my fault. Every two weeks, a check would arrive that was too small, my heart would sink and the same frustration would rise up in me. Finally, I called the accountant and asked her to check it.

"Thanks," I said weakly, "I'm sure it's my mistake, but . . ."

"No, those are the right amounts," she said.

"But I have down that I worked these days and these hours."

"You did," she said. "What's the problem?"

"At one hundred dollars an hour, that's not right."

"Oh," she laughed. "Well, you're figuring this up at the wrong rate. Why do you think you get a hundred dollars an hour? You make seventy. All the singers do."

"What? Trent guaranteed me one hundred dollars an hour with no future royalties."

"He would never pay a singer that much." She smirked. "He told me to pay you seventy dollars an hour like all the other girls get."

The way she said "girls" made me feel small and stupid. I didn't like that feeling.

"I need to talk to Trent," I said, my heart racing.

She transferred me and he picked up the phone. If I hadn't felt so angry and used, I would never have found the courage to even phone him. I kindly reminded him how much he had promised to pay me. When he laughed, I felt worse.

"Look," he said, "you're scheduled to sing Friday afternoon. Why don't you come over to the business office—we'll straighten out this misunderstanding."

Misunderstanding? That's what he called it?

Friday, I walked into the office complex and saw a new Jaguar parked in Trent's space. The atrium lobby was filled with waterfalls and tropical fish. I had no idea it would be so palatial. I grew more upset as I thought about my small, inaccurate paychecks.

"Trent will see you now," his secretary said.

"Hi! Come on in," he smiled.

I took the seat in front of him. Just then, he reached under his desk and pressed a button. The drapes closed electronically. He pressed another button and the door locked.

"There, that's better," he smiled. "Hold all my calls," he said, leaning into his speakerphone.

The "good girl" who never confronted a man in authority was ready to take this guy on.

"What's the next button you're going to push?" I said folding my arms.

"Does the floor open up and the piranha appear?"

He laughed in a phony sort way and I leaned forward, shouting in my mind not to be intimidated. I came to the point and reminded him what he promised to pay me when he hired me.

"Wow, I just don't remember saying that," he said evasively. "You see, none of the other singers get that and I just don't know why I ever would have promised you that much. Hey, even if I agree now to give you that, how would it look to them? What would I tell them?"

"What you pay other singers is none of my business," I said quickly. "I only know what I need to be paid and I can't work for less than the one hundred an hour you promised me."

"Hope, this is a tough business. You have no idea how much it costs to do this kind of production," he said, staring at me.

Tough business? I thought. *Jaguar? Waterfalls?*

I felt myself weakening. The old guilt rose up again. What others needed came before what I needed. I didn't count. I shouldn't inconvenience people.

I was lucky to even have a job. I was just a "woman."

Suddenly, I "woke up."

"I'm an experienced, talented singer," I proclaimed. "Whether you remember or not, we did agree on one hundred dollars an hour. It's way below what other national singers make with royalties, but I chose to work with you in this arrangement. This isn't about what you pay everyone else, it's about what you and I agreed upon."

"I just don't think that would be fair," he repeated.

"I sang those TV station tags." I began. "The ones going to every city."

"So?"

"I've only sung half of them. If you want me to finish them, I will—at one hundred dollars an hour."

Trent put his hands behind his head. "Oh, I get it." He laughed. Suddenly, he reached under his desk. The door clicked open. The drapes started moving.

"No problem," he said. "A hundred an hour it is, I just thought we should chat a bit."

I walked outside, put on my sunglasses and shouted, "Yes!"

Every two weeks my checks arrived for the right amounts, and I continued an enjoyable career there until I moved to another city.

I had been willing to lose everything in that meeting because I was finally tired of losing myself. I wasn't driving a Jaguar or going to a house filled with waterfalls. But as I drove my little Toyota down the freeway, I felt richer than I had ever felt in my life. I found something I had given up so many times, I thought it was gone forever:

my self-respect. And I was never going to lose it again.

Hope Faith

Key Words to Survival

In order to gain my life I had to lose it.

Carol Collopy

As a young mother, I thought having four children under the age of four was a challenge. That challenge pales, however, when compared with having two weddings, a mastectomy, and serving as hostess for my husband's business conference—all in two weeks.

Survival became the key word, followed in swift order by hurry and secrecy, along with support and humor.

In February 1980, two of our sons announced that they each wanted to be married in early June. They agreed on the first and third Saturdays. One wedding would be in Michigan, the other in Colorado.

Delighted that they had made happy commitments, we chorused, "Wonderful! It's fine with us."

"It even works well for the conference," added my husband. "We can stay in Colorado after the second wedding."

As president of the American Bankers' Association, he had major responsibilities in Colorado the third week of June. "I'll just take two suitcases," I added, thinking about my responsibilities as his hostess.

All went well until I discovered a small lump in my left breast three days before the first wedding. I hurried to my doctor who hurried me to X ray. From the moment he saw the X ray, *hurry* became a key word.

The doctors rushed me into surgery for a biopsy. As I came out from the anesthesia, the wavering lines of a shape formed into the young surgeon who had done the biopsy. Groggy, I barely comprehended his words. "Remove the breast tomorrow." I tried to shout, but it was just a whisper. "No! Not now! The weddings!"

The older doctor, a friend, explained the percentages of survival based on treatment, and how long it took to recover. Everyone hastened to tell me what I must do immediately.

Finally, I announced in what I hoped was a normal voice, "This is Thursday. I will not ruin the wedding. I will come home Sunday and you can operate on Monday."

Secrecy was added to the key-word list. Had I known my daughter-in-law as well then as I do now, I might have told her. But at the time, I would not announce such frightening news to her in the midst of such joy.

Although our son, the groom-to-be, was very worried, my husband and I swore him to secrecy. "Let's wait until after the celebration," we said. Then we drove to Michigan, held the rehearsal dinner, cried and smiled during the wedding and danced at the reception. Our insistence on leaving at dawn the next day, missing the special breakfast, caused some raised eyebrows, but it could not be helped.

I went to the hospital that evening, had surgery the following morning and awoke minus a breast—but free from cancer. No chemotherapy or radiation required.

Prayers and thanksgiving were very important to us at this time, but hurry became vital again. Rapid recovery was essential. The next wedding was in twelve days, and we had to drive to Colorado.

Support joined the key-word list. Friends and family supported me vigorously. They brought food and sent get-well cards. The just-married couple called from their honeymoon in Florida to thank us for not spoiling their wedding. The about-to-be-married couple in Colorado offered to change the date. But the conference could not be canceled. All had to proceed as planned.

With more prayers, thanks and all the fine support, I did begin the recovery process quickly. But other worries arose that, in retrospect, now seem trivial. How would I look? Unable to wear a prosthesis immediately, I worried about my appearance at this next wedding. How could I look like a mother of the groom? My dress would not fit properly.

Again, support. A friend who'd had a mastectomy the year before showed me how she'd used cotton and Kleenex to fill out and look balanced during the time before she could start wearing her prosthesis.

It is easy now to look back and laugh at this and the other little strategies we devised, but at the time, conquering each problem caused pain and seemed traumatic. I had not had time to grieve about my loss in private before events pressed me into the public eye at a major occasion of my life: our second son's marriage.

However, slowly, humor began to help us cope. My left arm could not reach my back. The first time my husband awkwardly worked at the fastener of my brassiere, we exploded with laughter as he commented, "Somehow, this isn't the same as it used to be." Pulling up my panty hose initially caused frustration then giggles then snorts of laughter as I squirmed and he tugged.

In Colorado, the key word from my family continued to be support, shown by their encouragement. While no one expressed pity, all of them built up my confidence. I could handle this happy occasion. A hug here, a pat and a smile, a chair conveniently placed nearby relieved fatigue and let me know how much someone cared. Later, I learned they'd promised each other not to pity me.

"We promised to be strong, so you would have to be," one of them told me years later.

The bride glowed with joy and gratitude at not having to change plans. The second son and his friends took over the rehearsal dinner, a relaxed picnic at which I could be a happy guest. I marched up the church aisle proudly, knowing that my dress hung appropriately. My husband and I shared the joy of this second wedding. Our dancing at the reception was limited, but I managed a dance with the groom and another with my husband. No one paid attention to my left arm hanging limply at my side. We all had more fun than I had thought possible.

Despite friends urging me to skip the conference, where my hostess duties might be very tiring, I was determined to go. By then, my husband had become an expert at brassiere fastening and helping with panty hose. I was adept at padding appropriately. And humor had become a habitual key word. To this day, I giggle when I squirm my way into a pair of panty hose. A banker's wife with whom I had become acquainted over the years offered to come to our hotel room any time I needed assistance with my hair. When conference duties kept my husband too busy to help me, she arrived energetically to fasten a pearl necklace, put in my pierced earrings or wash my hair. We became close friends, sharing stories of our children and of our fears and dreams. She taught me to relax with breathing techniques and to gain strength through visualization exercises. Our times together helped me survive and enjoy the conference. Most important, she helped me start the necessary grieving process so that I would eventually feel whole again. By the end of the conference, despite the hurry and emotion, I was beginning to put my mastectomy into perspective.

The words, from survival to hurry, from secrecy to support, stand out in my memory of those demanding weeks. Family and friends, prayers and thanksgiving, along with a growing sense of humor helped me resolve fears and grief. Recognizing and using key words made survival a reality.

Peg Sherry

Youthful Promises

We turn not older in years, but new every day.

Emily Dickinson

The water sparkles below me. Breezes blow through my hair. I am feeling young. The titillating promise of excitement, fun and more youthful feelings is only a ski-length away.

While on vacation with my husband and two sons, I wanted to rent a ski boat and make a day of it. I thought it was a grand idea. I was imagining myself actually being an active participant in this family experience instead of the same, tired old cheerleader Mom. Since hitting midlife, I sporadically become delusional. So it was I, who shamed my reluctant husband into renting the boat by calling him a middle-aged grouch with no sense of adventure and precious little time to still assert his male athletic prowess. That seemed to do it.

I was feeling unusually frisky and daring that morning as I tugged on the old swimsuit, not standing in front of a mirror, of course. I recalled the young girl of my early twenties. Ah, I was so cute, so tan, so skinny. I had once skied on a clear blue lake in Colorado. The sky so blue, the air so clean as I skimmed effortlessly along the surface of the water. I had the world at my feet. I was in control. I could do anything! The flood of exciting memories was quickly taking hold, smothering that one little nagging doubt. The doubt that whispered, "You only did this once?" But who cares for caution when the lure of the ski is calling? I was pumped! I was revved! I was ready! My husband could see the gleam in my eye, the determination to ski toward my youth. He knew there was nothing he could say to dissuade me. He only stood there slowly shaking his head.

The first minor detail to attend to is finding the right size life vest. After rummaging around the boat and trying on three or four, which were, of course, made for big strong men (who know how to ski), I finally found a cute little red vest that I thought looked pretty good on me, especially since it hid most of my body.

Next comes the part where I jump, however awkwardly, off the boat and into the water. This was my only moment of slight hesitation as I remembered the swarm of nasty-looking fish up by the dock. I had more pressing things to think about at the moment though. The boys were throwing skis at me. I began struggling to get those slender, very long skis on my feet, not an easy task when you're in the water with your cute little life vest having swollen up around your neck and continuously making you roll on your back. After accomplishing that unlady-like task, I was feeling pretty damn good about myself, feeling a little more empowered—a little more cocky, a little more back-to-the-middle of middle age.

Meanwhile, the guys are circling around me in the boat. Over the hum of the engine

I think I hear words. "Row-row!" Row? Why do they want me to row? I begin to move my arms in some sort of circular motion when my son leans way over the boat and screams "Rope!" Oh yes! The rope! Grab the rope as it comes around. I knew that. All I need to do is to find the rope that is floating out there somewhere in all that water. I don't see it, but the guys are yelling and pointing so I guess it's out there. I keep searching, searching. Paddling this way, paddling that way, spinning in circles looking for the rope. "Right there, Mom! Right there!" "Right where—WHERE?" Finally the boys throw the rope out where I can see it. I'm wondering why they didn't just do that in the first place.

Rope in hand, skis in a semi-upward direction, I nod my head like a professional, signaling "Good to go!" I'm sure I can do this. I did it once before, didn't I? The engine revs up, the propeller begins spinning. My husband, behind the wheel, full of trepidation, pulls back on the throttle and takes the boat slowly forward, his head bowed, in what I think is prayer.

We start slowly. I feel the rushing of the

water against my skin, surfacing the memories of yesteryear. Aaah, yes. I'm beginning to relax into this when the boat starts speeding up. I grip the rope a little tighter, remembering that I still need to get up out of the water. Suddenly we begin going very fast . . . faster . . . and now way too fast! I don't know what happened, but without warning, this sleek, shiny new ski boat has turned into a rip-roaring monster, twisting and turning, blazing through the water at breakneck speed. My mind is a complete blank. What am I supposed to do? There's no time to think. I just keep gripping the rope even as my arms are being ripped apart from the rest of my body! I do remember I'm supposed to keep my legs together—but, oh, the water. There's so much water! I don't remember this much water. Coming at me with the force of steel. I'm using every single muscle in these fifty-year-old legs, struggling to keep them together. Trying to maintain my balance, as well as a little dignity, I begin to come up—just a little more—and then . . . in a nano-second I feel it! Oh my God! My legs are actually coming apart—it's happening—it's—it's the splits!

The rope tears itself out of my clutches as if to say, "I've had enough of you," and leaves me to slam face down into what feels like a brick wall. Water immediately rushes up my nose and into my mouth. I think I may be drowning! Am I drowning? Is this it? Is this what will be in my obituary: "Drowned by splitting"? But then, I feel myself being buoyed up and rolled over on my back—Oh my dear, dear little red life vest!

Dazed and sputtering, I surface to find my family circling back towards me. They beg me to get back on the boat, which would have been the intelligent thing to do. But I couldn't let go of the dream just yet. After two more attempts, which were exact replicas of the first, I finally succumb to defeat. With resignation weighing heavy in my mind and heavier still in my body, I clumsily climb back on board, hitting my ankle on the propeller—the last humiliation. The monster's final way of saying, "Gotcha!"

While riding back to middle age, I look behind me, knowing I left my youth some-where out there in the wide expanse of blue water. A tear forms and rolls down my sunburned (slightly wrinkled) cheek. My mind knows it is time to say good-bye. My heart, well, my heart is heavy and sad.

My boys are already scrambling to jump in and begin their amazing acrobatics. As I watch them I feel my sad and heavy heart begin its slow and healing journey. It will take time, but somehow this cushy seat makes it a little more tolerable. I feel my bones relaxing and my skin soaking up the sun. Maybe, just maybe, there are a few perks that come with my much-resisted promotion. I may not have to struggle so hard anymore. Perhaps the hard raw action of youth is giving way to a softer, gentler gesture of age. I am being carried along by the waves of time and with that thought I collapse into an exhausted and most welcomed sleep.

Denise Fleming

Freedom

Quite a few women told me, one way or another, that they thought it was sex, not youth, that's wasted on the young.

Janet Harris

My husband and I pull away from the curb, and I look tearfully through the back window as my youngest child disappears into the yawning abyss of a college campus. How can I let her go? My baby, only eighteen years old, alone, halfway across the country. She tosses a wave in our direction and is gone.

My life is over. First, my son, Zack, left for school and now Nora. My nest is empty.

About fifty miles down the road, on the spur of the moment (a new concept!) my husband and I change our route and wind through the glorious Green Mountains of Vermont. We spend the rest of the day hiking and sleep that night in a charming bed-and-breakfast.

We do it without consulting our children. And we do it without the promise of a nearby amusement park, shopping mall or movie theater. (And we do it without the fear of anyone walking in!)

Et voilà! The end of my much-dreaded empty nest syndrome.

Now I'm convinced it's all a myth. A joke. A lie. If parents knew beforehand how delightful an empty nest really is, they'd be tossing teenagers out of their houses right and left.

I am a good mom, loving and nurturing. Sort of. I have to admit I wasn't wild about Candy Land or Suzuki violin, but I did it, and I did it well. And having devoted myself to my kids for so many years, I do occasionally have great moments of longing for those good old days.

But those moments pass the second I

glance down at my car's odometer, only fifty miles added each week instead of 354. Miles of driving to and from and back and forth to every game, dance, practice, lesson or meet. And the car insurance! Without teenagers on your insurance policy, you can save enough for a trek through Nepal or a Las Vegas vacation, losses included.

Yet another bonus: When I reach for my car keys, lo and behold, they're on the hook where I last left them. In fact, all my possessions are where I last left them: my brush, my tennis racquet, my yellow sweater, my books.

I do laundry only once a week now. I watch whatever I want on TV (the remote isn't lost), and last but not least, I listen to my own music! I sleep at night not worrying about where my children are or when they might come rolling in.

Everything changes, especially your relationships. If you're married, you can rediscover why you came together in the first place. You're less judgmental, less cautious, less concerned with what you say and do since it no longer affects the children.

If you want to begin a relationship now,

you might just find it easier to start one without the demands of your children coming (where else?) first. You might just discover a date prefers you with perfume instead of eau de peanut butter, and you will, I promise, discover the delight of finishing a sentence uninterrupted.

There is, as with everything, a downside to an empty nest. Those little fledglings have to fly and land somewhere, so you might need a second job to help furnish their landing pad, or to refurnish yours. Why? Because they will have carried off dishes, mops and the occasional table or chair. And if they're off to college, the cost is a killer—but the money saved on Froot Loops alone practically pays the tuition.

Since you no longer have to keep the household organized around the kids, your house can become an adult home, strewn with your own favorite toys and treasure. Oh, and if you've ever longed to sit for hours in meditation or dreamed of reading an entire book in one sitting, go for it right now.

Enjoy the freedom. It won't be long before that front door bursts open and

newly hatched chicks fly in calling,
"Grandma!"

Bonnie West

Scenes from a Marriage

Aging forces us to decide what is important in life.

Thomas Moore

We are standing in the kitchen glaring at one another. I remind my Valentine that he's officially taken over dishwasher duty, which means loading and unloading the old workhorse; that it's now 11:00 A.M.; and that, still, the clean dishes remain lodged inside while the dirty ones languish on the counter.

I avoid mentioning that in my dishwasher-loading/unloading era, the deed was always done early and that the platters were always standing like sentries on the bottom shelf, not leaning precariously on one another. These are fighting words on a Sunday morning. We both know it. But somehow, seconds later, we burst into laughter at our own foolishness. It's Sunday—and Valentine's Day—and what difference does it really make in the long run that the dishwasher isn't unloaded or that the platters aren't in perfect order?

At this stage of our union, we finally understand the futility of dumb arguments and while we still have them, of course, we end them sooner than we used to.

Score one for very married Valentines. Forget the plump red satin heart-shaped boxes of rich chocolate. Forget the love poems penned in passion, the wild embraces, the waltzes under crystal chandeliers. For some of us, Valentine's Day, even in all its commercial, hucksterish glory, remains a reminder that, in ordinary life, it's the little stuff that counts.

The notes left on the kitchen table in haste, signed with nicknames only we recognize. The way he remembers to pick up the exotic cheese I love, even though it means going miles out of his way. The fact that when it's raining and we're going out, he pulls the car right to the kitchen door for a presumably liberated lady.

Yes, those trifles, friends, count dearly in this season when we're reminded that love changes everything, conquers all, and makes the world go 'round.

I agree with all of the above. But I also know better.

In the autumn of a long and committed marriage, we celebrate love in quirky, not just cosmic, ways. I make chocolate pudding the old-fashioned way, the cooking, stirring, scorch-the-pot method, when I detect a certain sag to my beloved's shoulders, a certain weariness in his walk. And the fuss feels both right and rewarding.

On mornings when we both awaken not like songbirds but like terminal grouches, we deftly avoid conversation. And yes, it's a loving, not hostile, gesture. And in the sleepless dark, when the demons come, I know that I can reach over to a man who is soundly sleeping, gently wake him, and find myself in the homeland of his arms.

We haven't waltzed under a chandelier of any description in years, but every now and then, when the mood is right, my Valentine and I will dance around the kitchen to the strains of the radio, preferably to an old Frank Sinatra ballad. It's so corny that it's embarrassing, but we don't care. And some of our best moments—moments that bind and bond us and make our hearts leap— have come when we've stood in a silent, dark room and watched a grandchild sleeping.

It may not be classic romance. It may not meet the rapturous hype of magazines that speak of love as primal and wild, sensual and captivating. But for two late-middle-aged Valentines, those bedside vigils are an affirmation of loving long and well—loving right into the next generation.

So when the dishwasher eruptions come—and they always do—we rely on the best gifts of Valentinehood to get us though:

Humor.

Forgiveness.

Emotional generosity.

And a love that's old enough to have a burnished glow, but not too old to sparkle and to make two midlife Valentines enormously grateful for the gift of one another.

Sally Friedman

What Mothers Teach

Our power is just the force of our love for our children and grandchildren.

Barbara Weidner

Many years ago, when my daughter Sara was in the fifth grade, she came to me with a life-gripping problem. As tears welled up in her big brown eyes, she began explaining her dilemma.

"Marcy hates me!" she cried. "She hates me because Kathy is my friend, too. She wants me to be her friend and nobody else's." Sara choked back her tears and said, "She won't play with me if I hang out with Kathy. But, they are both my friends!"

I tried my mommy-best to console her and let her know that we cannot control how others feel and react. Even though we should understand feelings, there are some things that are out of our control, and some decisions we can only make for ourselves.

As I was trying to decide what motherly advice I could give her, she stumped me with, "You talk to Marcy. You tell her that I like her and want to be her friend, but I can have other friends, too!"

Oh boy. I sat there staring at her for a few moments trying to figure out how I got into this mess, when suddenly the idea came to me. I excused myself and left the room, telling her I would be right back. My mind raced. It was obvious that she needed to learn that there are just some things you need to do for yourself. Only, how could I teach her this without her feeling like I had failed her?

Picking up two wicker baskets from the living room, I quickly tossed their contents onto the floor and walked back into Sara's room. She stared at me like I was nuts.

"What are those for?" she asked with big, surprised eyes.

"It's a life lesson for you," I explained. "Just sit down and let me explain."

She sat on the edge of the bed with a wary eye. Placing the littler basket inside the big one, I placed the handle of the big basket over my arm and began to slowly walk around the room as I explained.

"When everyone is born, God gives them a little basket. This little one here is yours. The big one is mine. As you grow, so does the basket. But if you notice, your little basket is inside of mine. Why do you think that is?"

She just glared at me. Nope. Not getting through yet. Not even close.

I continued. "Your little basket is in mine because when you were born, there were too many things you couldn't do for yourself. I had the responsibility of feeding you, changing you, bathing you, and doing everything else you couldn't do on your own. So I put your basket in mine and carried them both for a while."

She nodded, but so far still thought I was crazy.

"Well, as you grew older and began to do some things on your own, I began placing a few more things in your basket. When you learned to tie your shoes, that went in your basket. You wouldn't want me tying your shoes now, would you?"

She bowed her head a second and said softly, "No, that would be stupid. I can tie my own shoes."

"Right," I said. "And when you learned how to put on your own clothes, I put that in your basket. You don't even like me telling you what to wear now, never mind dressing you."

She agreed with a small nod.

"As you grow older, there will be more and more things you must do on your own." As I spoke, I gradually took her basket out of mine and handed it to her. "You will eventually carry your own basket with things only you can do, like deciding who you want to be friends with, who you will date, what college you will go to, who you will marry."

She looked up at me and said, "I understand. There are some things that I have to do for myself because they are in my basket."

Hallelujah! The light came on! "Yes," I squealed, "but it's even better than that because you decide the things that belong in your basket or someone else's. Like now, you decide who you want to be friends with. If Marcy doesn't like your decision and gets angry, whose basket needs to carry her anger?"

She smiled. "Marcy's. Right?"

I hugged her and continued with the story. "You're absolutely right. Marcy's responses aren't in your basket. They are in hers. Now, one last thing you need to understand before the basket story is over." She was smiling big now and really getting into my little skit.

I stood there for a moment, thinking of my own mother and grandmother who were living with us, reminiscing about the things they used to do for me that now I do for them. Even though it tugged at my heart strings, I held up the big basket and said, "One day when I'm much older, there will be things I can no longer carry in my basket. When that time comes, eventually you will begin taking things out of my basket and placing them into your own. Just like I do now for Grandma and Momma. Eventually, the things that are in my basket will be taken out, for I won't always be strong enough to carry everything I'm carrying right now."

I reached over and gently took the small basket from her hands and traded with her. As she felt the large handle of the big basket and watched me take the little one, she understood.

Softly, I said, "Life is a circle."

As she smiled and gave me a big hug, she said, "Mom, I think I can put much more in my basket. Don't worry about Marcy. I can do this."

As I put the magazines and the potpourri back into the baskets in the living room, my own mother entered and asked me what I was doing. Smiling, I gave her a quick overview of my impromptu skit, feeling quite smug and proud of myself. Mom just smiled.

A few days later, I was surprised to see one of the tiniest baskets I've ever seen, sitting on the top of my computer desk. It was small enough to hide in the palm of my hand. Underneath it was a note, in my mother's handwriting that said simply, "Just remember, your basket isn't nearly as big as you think it is. Love, Mom."

Ferna Lary Mills

Who Called the Sheriff?

The capacity to care is the thing that gives life its deepest meaning and significance.

Pablo Casals

When my twin sons, Chad and Brad, were born, I was concerned about everything. Was the formula too hot or too cold? Was I doing everything right? Could I actually be the mother that two little boys needed? I wanted the world to be perfect for them.

Five years later, our little girl, Becky, completed our family. Would she get enough of my undivided attention? Would the boys feel neglected by the amount of time a new baby required? I wanted everybody to be healthy and happy. I worked hard to see that they were.

As the kids grew older, I worried about tonsils, earaches, throat infections and many other common childhood illnesses. I worried about their future heartaches. I didn't want anybody to make them sad. I wanted to protect them with all the strength I had.

I didn't like it when the boys spent time "warming the bench" during Little League and midget-football games. I wondered if they felt inferior because of their smaller size. I worried about Becky when she missed the ball when she played softball. I was afraid she wouldn't make it during flag tryouts.

Many times the kids told me not worry. "Everything will be fine," they constantly reminded me. But like most moms, I worried anyway.

Before long, the teen years were upon us. I sat up late at night waiting for the boys to return home. I worried about drunk drivers on the road. I worried about how the boys would react if one of their friends did something wrong. If they were five minutes late, I panicked. Many times the thought crossed my mind that I would call the sheriff if they weren't home on time. Luckily, they always arrived home safe and sound before I had to resort to such measures.

"Please don't ever call the sheriff," one of the boys said when I threatened him after a late arrival.

The day the boys moved away to attend college was a sad day indeed. I worried about the kinds of professors they would have. Would they make good grades in school? Would they ever graduate? I worried about them being able to take care of themselves and actually cook their own meals. Would they starve?

A few months after the boys left for college, our doorbell rang in the middle of the night. It startled us when we looked at the clock and saw that it was three o'clock in the morning. "Something must be wrong," I shouted to my husband, Roy, as we both jumped up. We ran to the door, opened it and there stood a deputy sheriff.

"You need to call your sons," he sternly announced. I picked up the telephone, but unfortunately, it was dead. A line outside had been accidentally cut. Roy and I jumped into the car and took off to the nearest telephone. My stomach ached with middle-aged worry. My husband was shaking so badly that he could barely dial the number.

On the first ring, Chad answered the telephone. "What's wrong?" Roy shouted into the receiver.

"We were worried about you," Chad told him. "We've been trying to call you all night, and you didn't answer. We called the sheriff's office and asked them to go check on you."

Chad then asked to speak to me. "I was so worried, Mama," he confessed.

"Don't worry, son," I said. "Everything will be fine." For the first time in their lives, the table was turned and the boys were worried about us. And to top it off, they were the ones who actually resorted to calling the sheriff.

Nancy B. Gibbs

What Do You Have to Say for Yourself?

Memory is more indelible than ink.
Anita Loos

My dad died recently. I expected it; after all, he was eighty-six years old. He had emphysema and his heart was failing. His hands, ravaged by arthritis, could no longer grasp his coffee cup. I had not lived near him for over twenty-five years—I had my own life, four grown children, a busy career, a happy marriage, a house full of dogs.

I often heard friends talk about losing their parents. They talked about the pain of it, the loneliness, feelings of being lost without them. I thought, *But that won't be me.* I knew I would miss him, and I would surely be sorry he was gone. But lost without him? After all, what did he really provide me these days in the way of guidance or support? I had been self-sufficient for a long time. Oh, I talked to him every week, but those calls were for his reassurance, to let him know we were fine. He hardly understood the world my brother and I live in. He couldn't understand our jobs, why we flew all over the world. It wasn't that he didn't know anything about the world. Even at his age, his eyes were good and his mind was sound. He read three papers a day. He knew the political landscape better than most anyone I knew. But his children's lives always seemed beyond his comprehension.

He would begin every Saturday's call with, "Well, what do you have to say for yourself?" And every Saturday, I would have to recount what I had done, what the kids had done, where I had traveled. I also had to be up on the latest in Washington politics, know whether the Green Bay Packers had won, and preferably, who they had recently traded. It would be helpful if I was up on all recent news events, and it would really be best if I had a strong opinion about something.

I'll admit it now, sometimes I found these calls exasperating. But I realize now that this question has been a part of my life since I could speak. I remember walking home from school, knowing my dad would be there, the question on his lips. And I would sometimes dawdle a little on the way, trying to think of an answer. Had I done something clever? Had I read something interesting?

Maybe the question was just a way to open a conversation. Maybe he just wanted to know how my day had gone. But now I realize it took on much greater meaning to me.

I felt that, every day, my dad was asking me to account for myself. What was I doing? And why was I doing it? Knowing this question was coming made me think more about what I did, what I wanted, what I cared about. Even his questions about our jobs now seem not a lack of understanding on his part, but rather an implicit question about whether this was really how we wanted to spend our time.

As I got older, there were times when my

dad asked, "Well, what do you have to say for yourself?" and I would respond, "Nothing."

His eyebrows would shoot up and he would look at me over his reading glasses. Then he would say, "Nothing?"

And I would swallow hard, nod my head, and repeat, "Nothing."

He would look me up and down then respond with an exaggerated, "Mmmm . . ." Then he would shrug his shoulder in that big John Wayne-way of his and change the subject. But as he moved on to ask me about Jim's latest fishing trip or Jen's job or Brooke's college or Dan's girlfriend or Zach's latest book, I knew I had disappointed him. And that was hard to take.

Now there are no more phone calls. I am feeling a little lost. And I am finding myself wanting to answer the question "What do you have to say for yourself?"

Today no one asks me to account for myself. Certainly not my husband, not my children. At the age of fifty, I can do what I want. There's no one there on Saturday to check on what I am up to, no one to wait for the answer on whether my latest book is done or why I haven't done that Habitat for Humanity work I said I would do. Not that Dad ever asked those things outright, either. But wrapped inside the "Big Question" were many implicit little ones.

Now, without my father acting as my compass in the world, I am faced with a greater test. I must go on, remembering that, though no one is asking, I must still account for myself and my actions. Will I become a slug without his weekly question? I hardly think so. But will an occasional Saturday go by when I feel I have been let off the hook, just a little? Probably.

So today, in honor of my dad, I would like to take another opportunity to account for myself.

What do I have to say for myself?

I say that I love deeply and am loved.

I know how to think clearly and act on what I believe.

I know how to set my priorities.

And when I see my children, I now always ask them, "Well, what do you have to say for yourself?"

Thanks, Dad.

Kate Rowinski

A Mother Sings

Life can only be understood backward but it must be lived forward.

Soren Kierkegaard

Jill paused halfway down our front steps. She turned and said, "Mom, will you sing to me? Will you hold me and sing like you used to when I was a little girl?" Her husband and her two little stepdaughters stopped and looked back.

I always sang to my kids when they were young. Jill and her older brother shared a bedroom, and I knelt between them, holding one's hand and stroking the blond head of the other. I sang and crooned through "Dona, Dona" and "Kumbaya." I swayed in rhythm to "Swing Low, Sweet Chariot." I never missed a verse of "Hush, Little Baby." I made up songs, too, a habit that drove my husband crazy. On nights when I was out, the kids begged, "Sing 'The Horse Broke the Fence,' Daddy," or "No, we want 'The Big Wheel' song." And they didn't mean "Proud Mary," which he might have managed, although he really couldn't carry a tune even when he knew the words.

But the kids and I always finished with "All Things Bright and Beautiful," as I watched their active bodies quiet and their eyes grow dreamy as they imagined the purple-headed mountains and ripe fruit in the garden of the old hymn. By the time I warbled my way through the refrain for the last time, one of them had usually twitched and fallen asleep.

As Jill grew from child to adult, it became apparent that she had inherited her father's trouble carrying a melody. She cuddles with her girls every night and she reads to them, but she just can't sing to them.

Recently, I baby-sat for our granddaughters. After I tucked them into our king-size bed, I sang "Dona, Dona," "Kumbaya," and all the others. Hannah, the six-year-old, lay still as a stone, gazing at the ceiling. Four-year-old Brianna came forward onto her hands and knees, staring into my eyes from so close that her features blurred. In the dim light coming through the open door, I saw her lips parted, glistening. Trance-like, she held perfectly still, listening as if she wanted to inhale the songs directly from my mouth.

It was a few days later Jill asked me to once again sing to her. She said, "The girls talked about your singing, Mom, and it brought back all the wonderful memories. I remember my cool pillow and your hand on my hair. I remember my nightgown with the sunbonnet dolls on it and the pink ice-cream cone quilt you made. Sometimes I would wake up when you kissed me one last time."

That's when she turned and asked, "Mom, will you sing to me, again?"

Her husband stood beneath the street lamp with a child balanced on each hip. Her father and brothers stood behind me, illuminated by the porch light. She's very tall, this girl of mine. Standing on the step below me, she still had to stoop to put her head against my chest. I wrapped my fingers in her long hair, and she wound her arms around my waist.

"What shall I sing, Jill?" I asked.

"You know, Mom," she said, looking up and smiling.

"'All Things Bright and Beautiful'?"

"Of course." She snuggled closer. "All the verses."

I kissed the top of her head and began to sing.

Swallowing a lump in my throat and stroking her back, I continued through the verses. Off-key, she joined in.

She began to cry, and so did I, but the words still flowed from my mouth as my mind drifted back over the years. I remembered her birth, how ecstatic I was to have a daughter—what an easy child she was. I remembered how she loved to please others—and still does. This girl who married young and took on the daunting task of raising another woman's children is no longer under my wing. She's a young woman now, and I can't tuck the ice-cream cone quilt around her shoulders each night. I can't protect her from pain, from hurt and from mature responsibility. I can't make growing up any easier for her.

Jill's tears soaked through my T-shirt that night and mine dropped onto her bowed head. She clung tightly and then looked up into my face.

"The purple-headed mountains. Don't forget the purple-headed mountains," she whispered, staring at me through the dim light, just as Brianna had a few nights earlier, drinking in the words, the memories, the song. Drinking in my love.

My voice cracked, and I could sing no more. We stood locked together on the stairs. I know the enormity of the task she's taken on is sometimes almost more than she can handle. I know how hard she's working to create a home.

Cradling her in maternal love, allowing her to remember falling asleep to a mother's singing, was the best I could offer my daughter this night. Jill squeezed me tightly and then turned toward her husband and her stepdaughters. Her dad hugged me as we watched her settle the girls into the back seat of their car—and then I heard the hymn again. I strained my ears, listening. Jill was still humming the refrain. Then Brianna's thin, little child's voice burbled from the open car window as they pulled away from the curb: "All things wise and wonderful, the Lord God made them all."

Peggy Vincent

In One Split Second

In the depth of winter, I finally learned that there was in me an invincible summer.

Albert Camus

I had settled into my life. My oldest daughter had just moved away from home to attend college, my son was a junior in high school and my youngest daughter was in seventh grade. My husband of twenty-three years and I had just done some soul-searching and decided we were ready for a change in our careers and wanted to work together, so we opened a closet-designing business in the spring of 2000. It was coming home from work on a rainy night in

December that my life suddenly changed. I was looking forward to going home, getting into some warm, comfortable clothes, turning on some holiday music, lighting the Christmas tree and having a hot cup of tea before starting dinner.

I was rounding the bend in front of my daughter's middle school when I was hit head-on by a young girl who had been driving only a few months. She was coming down a hill and around a curve when she lost control of her car. I never saw it coming. The only part of the accident that I do remember is looking out the window into the rain and giving a woman my husband's cell-phone number. It would be a week before I was aware of anything else.

My first moments of awareness are still foggy. I didn't realize it, but I had been in a coma for a week. It was comforting to have my family at my side when I awoke. It was then that I learned about the accident. But I also had some information to share with my family. Although I had been unconscious, I had had a conversation with God during that first week in the hospital.

I was being wheeled into a room for some

procedure when I spotted the light. It was only an overhead fluorescent light, but looking into the light I heard THE VOICE. The skeptics in my life have offered their opinions of whom I was talking to (probably the doctor or a nurse), but I know it was God. He told me that I would be okay. I asked if I was going to die, and he assured me in these exact words, "YOU WILL LIVE AND BE IN HEAVEN." When I questioned him—I thought you had to die to go to heaven—he replied, "I'M SENDING YOU BACK TO YOUR FAMILY, AND THAT IN ITSELF IS HEAVEN." Oh, how right he is.

Once I was finally awake, my family was trying to be strong for me and doing what they could to comfort me. And there I was trying to comfort my family, telling them that I knew I would be okay because God had spoken to me. What I didn't know was the extent of my injuries.

I had broken my left foot, my left leg and both wrists. I had lacerated my right knee and left elbow. My lungs had collapsed, my spleen and intestines had ruptured and my right foot had done a 360-degree turn, crushing all the bones in my ankle.

According to my doctor, I was lucky to be alive.

I was released from the hospital on Christmas Eve and arrived home to find my home aglow with lights. My family had set up a bedroom for me in our family room so that I could be close to all the activity. I would be bedridden for the next four months, but with the help of my wonderfully devoted husband and three children, I slowly recovered. This whole experience pulled our family together in a way that was pure testimony to our love for one another. I was also blessed to have a full-time, dedicated nurse and a compassionate but no-nonsense physical therapist. I had to learn to use my hands again and first stand then walk again. The pain was overwhelming, but God answered my prayers for help every time without fail.

For the four months that I was bedridden, every Monday, Wednesday and Friday night my wonderful friends and neighbors provided a full meal from soup to nuts to my family.

I am now in my eleventh month of recovery, and through ongoing physical therapy, I am learning how to walk again. I can't bend my ankle, so some of the activities I loved to do will probably no longer be part of my life—gardening, tennis, camping and driving a car will be severely limited. Even the ability to do my job has been seriously restricted. But I am okay with that. It has given me a chance to reflect on my priorities, to reevaluate what is important and what I want to do with the rest of my life. What difference can I make? I have always enjoyed life; I feel blessed. But now it is even more important that nothing is ever taken for granted again. I have not felt even a moment of anger or resentment or questioned, Why me? God allowed me the peace of mind right from the beginning—that everything would be okay. And it is.

At this stage of my life, I am ready for a new challenge. What I have been through will not change. So I have only to go forward and make the best of it. Life for any of us can change in just one split second. It's how we deal with it that makes the outcome either a disaster or an opportunity. Personally, I am looking forward to the next chapter of my life—certainly less physical but probably more rewarding.

Cecelia Albanese

Rules for Paging,
Rules for Aging

After fifty most of the bullshit is gone.

Isabel Allende

We didn't intend to come up with rules when the three of us decided to share our writing. We were all over fifty and thought we could be free of rules. We'd followed them all. Now we wanted to shed them, like we'd shed girdles in the sixties.

So, when we started our writer's group, we decided to work without constricting guidelines. We'd have free-form meetings. But after floundering around for a while, we gave up this anarchy, realizing some rules were needed if we were to take our writing seriously.

Only later did we come to see that these rules worked in other areas of our lives, as well. We're learning to navigate a new stage of life, just the three of us, meeting every other Monday with short stories, plays, mysteries and memoirs—and our rules.

Rule 1: START WITH THE GOOD STUFF

When we critique each other's work, there are frequently red marks all over the pages. To make this medicine easier to take, we start each critique with what is good about the piece. Then, with the writer basking in the glow of hearing how skillful her writing is, the not-so-positive stuff can be discussed.

If there is any rule that applies to aging, this is it. The papers and television news are full of the problems of aging—fading memories, fatal illnesses, scams to cheat the trusting. But what if we started by thinking about what we gain from getting older, not what we lose? Like a new sense of time. When we were raising our kids, we always looked ahead to each new stage, to when our babies would crawl, talk, walk, feed themselves, get out of diapers, get into school.

Now we know how fast the chipmunk-cheeked face of the nursing baby sharpens into the schoolgirl's studious look. And we realize that, with each change, the special world each face inhabits disappears, too. So, we take the time to value what the world presents to us, through the eyes of our grandchildren and through our own more understanding eyes.

Rule 2: BELIEVE IN THE POSSIBILITIES OF THE PIECE

Writing, like life, is not a goal but a process. And, as in life, it is easy to give up. The excuses are legion. It's too difficult to write; the storyline isn't working; I don't know where it's taking me. But if we don't trust the possibility that it will work out, we'll never get it written. And if those who read our work don't look for the possibilities, their doubts can discourage us from finishing it. So, we look for the possibilities of each idea, each piece of work.

Just as we look for the potential in aging. Not that growing older in our society is easy. The emphasis on staying young—no matter what it takes or costs—is strong. It's sometimes hard to find the upside of getting old.

But as mature women we have endless possibilities, from the sublime to the silly: never wearing panty hose again; wearing big, dangling rhinestone earrings with jeans; eating dessert first—or eating dessert only; going back to graduate school for the sheer joy of learning; taking up glassblowing—or skydiving. We can do what we want. It's all possible.

Rule 3: PRESENT YOUR WORK WITHOUT EXPLANATIONS OR APOLOGIES

What has been written in solitude is not easily presented to a group. There is a temptation to explain it away, to discount our work as unimportant. This rule means never saying we're sorry for what we've written.

It's harder to do sometimes, with our lives. We look back, rethink decisions. Should I have married him? Should I have gone back to school? Why didn't I take that job in Duluth? Why did (or didn't) I have children?

But who we are is the sum of all our life

decisions. Change one decision and the whole thing falls apart like the plot of a story unravels when a character is changed. Perhaps the story of our life isn't what we started out to write. It doesn't matter. It is special because it's ours. We present our lives—and our work—as we've written them, without excuses or explanations.

Rule 4: IT'S YOUR STORY AND YOU CAN DO ANYTHING WITH IT YOU LIKE

Often when our work is seen through another's eyes, we see the holes in our thinking, the mistakes in our grammar, the confusion in our explanations. But sometimes it's hard to understand why the group doesn't get it. This rule reminds us that even though we solicited the advice, we don't have to take it.

Women of our generation have frequently led their lives listening to voices other than their own. Following the guidance of parents, teachers or spouses, they let their own dreams sleep quietly in their hearts. Now, as we get older, we can listen to our own voices, still hearing the viewpoints of others, but doing with our lives what we want to do. To write, to sing, to dance, to gain control

of our time and talents, in spite of and without regard to—sometimes even contrary
to—what others expect of us. It's our story
and we'll write the second half the way we
want to.

*Rule 5: LISTENING CAN BE AS IMPOR-
TANT AS PROBLEM SOLVING*

Sometimes a writer just needs a listener.
For example, one of us needed to vent her
frustration when a hoped-for mentor
showed no interest in her writing. It was
enough that we listened to her and read her
unsent venomous letters. And when one of
us faced a public reading of her story about
red lingerie and sex on the kitchen floor,
talking about her feelings let her go forth
with confidence. We've come to realize that
a writing-associated problem may come up
time after time—the ongoing revisions of a
play, the problem of finding time to write—
precisely because there are no easy or uni-
form solutions.

Just like in our lives. We provide a shoulder but not a solution for frustrations with
kids, husbands, grandchildren and computer programs, as well as writing. But then,
we've always known about the listening

rule. Women are good at it.

Rule 6: END WITH THE GOOD STUFF

We begin critiques with good stuff, and we end them positively, too, not wanting to leave critical words hanging in the air. And as we close our notebooks at the end of our meetings, we always express how glad we are to have been together.

Frequently we exchange e-mails after our meetings about how helpful a critique was, or how inspiring someone's hard work was or how the group's support helped one of us keep going with her writing.

The longer we live, the more we know about hurts and sadness in our own lives and in the world. But we know more, too, about the joys and beauty. Why not end each day, then, with a recounting of what went right that day? And each time we leave those we care about, we can leave them a positive word, a gift of the good stuff, until we see them again.

Jane Mozena, Ginny Foster and Peggy Bird

It's Never Too Late To . . .

Act on our dreams.
Be what you want to be.
Change your future.
Do things differently.
Enrich others' lives.
Face your fears.
Get out of neutral.
Have fun.
Initiate friendships.
Jumpstart possibilities.
Knock the "t" off can't.
Live enthusiastically.
Make a difference.
be Nonjudgmental.
Orchestrate your legacy.
Plan for tomorrow.
Question your priorities.
Reinvent yourself.

Stop keeping score.
Take a leap of faith.
Uncork your mind.
Value who you are.
Wake up your luck.
eXplore your spirituality.
Yearn for fulfillment.
Zoom in on love.

Meiji Stewart

More Chicken Soup?

We enjoy hearing your reactions to the stories in *Chicken Soup for the Soul* books. Please let us know what your favorite stories were and how they affected you.

Many of the stories and poems you enjoy in *Chicken Soup for the Soul* books are submitted by readers like you who had read earlier *Chicken Soup for the Soul* selections.

We invite you to contribute a story to one of these future volumes.

Stories may be up to 1,200 words and must uplift or inspire. To obtain a copy of our submission guidelines and a listing of upcoming *Chicken Soup* books, please write, fax or check our Web sites.

Chicken Soup for the Soul
P.O. Box 30880
Santa Barbara, CA 93130
fax: 805-563-2945
Web site: *www.chickensoup.com*

Peace Through the Magic of Story

In the spirit of giving voice to peace for American adults and children, a portion of each sale of the original edition, *Chicken Soup to Inspire a Woman's Soul* , is donated to **Peace Tales**, a nonprofit organization that produces compact disc recordings that give lessons in peacemaking to American audiences through the magic of story.

The first such production, "Holding Up the Sky: Peace Tales for Kids" (©2003) features New Mexico school social worker and storyteller Sarah Malone. The fifty-six-minute CD includes multicultural stories, music and poetry that provide peaceful approaches to typical conflicts like jealousy, teasing and bullying. Author/storyteller Joe Hayes calls the recording a "weapon of mass instruction!" One hundred percent of the proceeds benefit peace causes: children affected by armed conflict overseas (through The Women's Commission for Refugee Women & Children) and Peace Talks Radio, a New Mexico radio forum for nonviolence and peacemaking.

Further information on Peace Tales is available at: *www.peacetales.org* and *www.womenscommission.org*.

Who Is Jack Canfield?

Jack Canfield is one of America's leading experts in the development of human potential and personal effectiveness. He is both a dynamic, entertaining speaker and a highly sought-after trainer. Jack has a wonderful ability to inform and inspire audiences toward increased levels of self-esteem and peak performance.

Jack currently has three wonderful horses living in his stable and rides with his wife Inga, his son Christopher, and his step-daughter Riley.

In addition to the *Chicken Soup for the Soul* series, Jack has coauthored numerous books, including his most recent release, *The Success Principles, How to Get From Where You Are to Where You Want to Be* with Janet Switzer, *The Aladdin Factor* with Mark Victor Hansen, *100 Ways to Build Self-Concept in the Classroom* with Harold C. Wells, *Heart at Work* with Jacqueline Miller and *The Power of Focus* with Les Hewitt and Mark Victor Hansen. He is regularly seen on television shows such as *Good Morning America, 20/20* and *NBC Nightly News.* For further information about Jack's books, tapes and training programs, or to schedule him for a presentation, please contact:

Self-Esteem Seminars
P.O. Box 30880
Santa Barbara, CA 93130
phone: 805-563-2935 • fax: 805-563-2945
Web site: *www.chickensoup.com*

Who Is Mark Victor Hansen?

In the area of human potential, no one is better known and more respected than Mark Victor Hansen. For more than thirty years, Mark has focused solely on helping people from all walks of life reshape their personal vision of what's possible. .

He is a sought-after keynote speaker, bestselling author and marketing maven. Mark is a prolific writer with many bestselling books such as *The One Minute Millionaire, The Power of Focus, The Aladdin Factor* and *Dare to Win,* in addition to the *Chicken Soup for the Soul* series.

Mark has appeared on *Oprah,* CNN and *The Today Show,* and has been featured in *Time, U.S. News & World Report, USA Today, New York Times* and *Entrepreneur* and countless radio and newspaper interviews.

As a passionate philanthropist and humanitarian, he has been the recipient of numerous awards that honor his entrepreneurial spirit, philanthropic heart and business acumen for his extraordinary life achievements, which stand as a powerful example that the free enterprise system still offers opportunity to all.

Mark Victor Hansen & Associates, Inc.
P.O. Box 7665
Newport Beach, CA 92658
phone: 949-764-2640 • fax: 949-722-6912
FREE resources online at:
www.markvictorhansen.com

Who Is Stephanie Marston?

Stephanie Marston is an internationally published author, acclaimed speaker and life-quality expert. Stephanie is a licensed Marriage, Family Therapist with more than twenty-five years' experience in women's issues and parenting. Ms. Marston has appeared on numerous radio and television programs such as *The Oprah Winfrey Show*, *The Early Show*, and *Women-to-Women*.

Stephanie is one of the most sought-after experts in the country on a host of life-quality and family issues, especially how to balance life's competing priorities and create a high-quality life. She has conducted seminars for more than 50,000 women, parents, and mental health professionals internationally. Stephanie delivers keynote addresses, seminars and workshops to women's organizations, corporations, parent groups, professional conferences, associations and the general public.

For further information about Stephanie's books, tapes and programs, or to schedule her for a presentation, please contact:

Life Quality Seminars
Box 31453
Santa Fe, NM 87594-1453
Phone: 505-989-7596 • fax: 505-989-4486
Web site: *www.stephaniemarston.com*

Contributors

If you would like to contact any of the contributors for information about their writing or would like to invite them to speak in your community, look for their contact information included in their biography.

Cecelia Albanese, the mother of three, married her high school sweetheart Sal. She moved from Philadelphia to Atlanta thirteen years ago. Being published for the first time has encouraged her to continue writing. She also enjoys reading, painting, arts and crafts and traveling with her husband in their RV. She can be reached at *cecelia13@charter.net.*

Peggy Bird lives in Vancouver, Washington. Her writing has appeared in such publications as *The Christian Science Monitor, Collectors News, Miniature Quilts* and *Clay Times.* Most recently her work was included in the anthologies *Dear Mom* and *A Christmas Collection.* She can be reached via e-mail at: *friedbird@juno.com.*

Ginny Foster, a retired high-school teacher from Portland, Oregon, has returned to her first love, writing. She has won national and regional awards for play writing. Her e-mail address is *gingame@portland.quik.com*.

Sally Friedman, an essayist from New Jersey, is a graduate of the University of Pennsylvania who writes for newspapers and magazines. The mother of three daughters, the grandmother of six and the wife of a retired judge, she is an admitted workaholic and chocaholic.

Nancy B. Gibbs is a pastor's wife, mother and grandmother. The author of *Celebrate Life . . . Just for Today*, she is also a weekly religion columnist and freelance writer. Her stories have appeared in numerous books and magazines. She has contributed several stories to the *Chicken Soup for the Soul* series. Contact her at *Daiseydood@aol.com*.

Mary Clare Lockman is a registered nurse in a busy Oncology/Hospice Unit. She also enjoys spending time with family and friends, reading, traveling and writing. "Paper Suits Me" is an excerpt from her book, *Warning! Family Vacations May Be Hazardous to Your Health*. She can be reached at (651) 646-7984; or *mclockman@msn.com*.

Ferna Lary Mills is the director of Rainbow Faith, a Christian grief ministry, and author of *The Rainbow: Words of Inspiration, Faith and Hope*.

Many of Ferna's poems and stories have been published in various magazines and anthologies. Reach her at (903) 445-0915 or by e-mail at *ferna@rainbowfaith.com*.

Jane Mozena lives in Portland, Oregon, where she writes short fiction and personal essays. Her work has been seen in *Holiday Tales* and *Dear Mom, Letters of Love, Loss and Longing*, and her short story *"The Dissection"* won an award in the 1999 Clark College Fiction Contest.

Kate Rowinski is a writer and consultant. Her credits include a number of children's books as well as several books of non-fiction for adults. Kate and her husband, Jim, have four grown children who have left the nest. Their numerous dogs, who have chosen not to leave the nest, live with them in Charlottesville, Virginia.

Peg Sherry, a "closet" writer for years, invested her energies in family and academia: four children, master's degree, teaching regular and gifted students at all levels, including college. Upon retiring, she focused on submitting her writings. Her work is in local and state magazines and in her published books of poems and essays. E-mail: *mtsherry@aol.com*.

Peggy Vincent is author of a memoir, *Baby Catcher: Chronicles of a Modern Midwife* (Scribner 2002). After "catching" nearly 3,000 babies as a Berkeley, California, midwife, Peggy is now a full-time writer. She lives in Oakland with her husband and teenaged son; two older children live nearby. Contact: *PV@peggyvincent.com.*

Bonnie West has written essays and articles for national magazines. Her first love is fiction. She teaches yoga and has stretching and relaxation audiotapes and CDs available. She has also made a "Relax into Writing" CD. She can be e-mailed at *yogabonnie@yahoo.com.*

Take time for you.

Code #1541 • $14.95

Code #0448 • $14.95

Also Available

Chicken Soup African American Soul
Chicken Soup Body and Soul
Chicken Soup Bride's Soul
Chicken Soup Caregiver's Soul
Chicken Soup Cat and Dog Lover's Soul
Chicken Soup Christian Family Soul
Chicken Soup Christian Soul
Chicken Soup College Soul
Chicken Soup Country Soul
Chicken Soup Couple's Soul
Chicken Soup Expectant Mother's Soul
Chicken Soup Father's Soul
Chicken Soup Fisherman's Soul
Chicken Soup Girlfriend's Soul
Chicken Soup Golden Soul
Chicken Soup Golfer's Soul, Vol. I, II
Chicken Soup Horse Lover's Soul
Chicken Soup Inspire a Woman's Soul
Chicken Soup Kid's Soul
Chicken Soup Mother's Soul, Vol. I, II
Chicken Soup Nature Lover's Soul
Chicken Soup Parent's Soul
Chicken Soup Pet Lover's Soul
Chicken Soup Preteen Soul, Vol. I, II
Chicken Soup Single's Soul
Chicken Soup Soul, Vol. I-VI
Chicken Soup at Work
Chicken Soup Sports Fan's Soul
Chicken Soup Teenage Soul, Vol. I-IV
Chicken Soup Woman's Soul, Vol. I-II

Available wherever books are sold.
For a complete listing or to order direct:
Telephone (800) 441-5569 • Online www.hcibooks.com
Prices do not include shipping and handling. Your response code is CCS.